CONTENTS

ISBN: 978-1-4803-6319-9

WALT DISNEY MUSIC COMPANY
WONDERLAND MUSIC COMPANY, INC.

DISTRIBUTED BY

HAL•LEONARD®
CORPORATION

7777 W. BLUEMOUND RD. P.O. BOX 13819 MILWAUKEE, WI 53213

Disney characters and artwork © Disney Enterprises, Inc.

Unauthorized copying, arranging, adapting, recording, Internet posting, public performance,
or other distribution of the printed music in this publication is an infringement of copyright.
Infringers are liable under the law.

In Australia Contact:
Hal Leonard Australia Pty. Ltd.
4 Lentara Court
Cheltenham, Victoria, 3192 Australia
Email: ausadmin@halleonard.com.au

Visit Hal Leonard Online at
www.halleonard.com

The Black Pearl

from Walt Disney Pictures' PIRATES OF THE CARIBBEAN:
THE CURSE OF THE BLACK PEARL

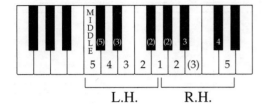

Music by Klaus Badelt

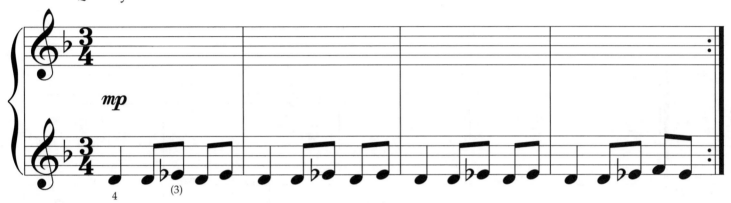

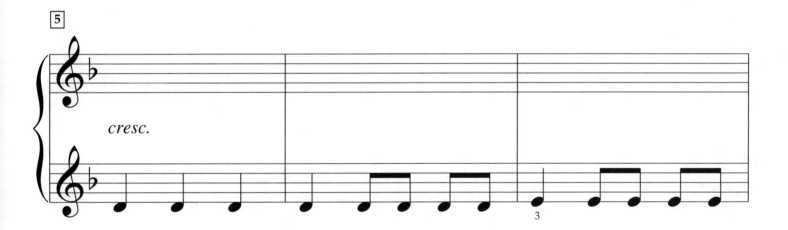

Duet Part (Student plays as written.)

© 2003 Walt Disney Music Company
All Rights Reserved   Used by Permission

Blood Ritual/
Moonlight Serenade

from Walt Disney Pictures' PIRATES OF THE CARIBBEAN:
THE CURSE OF THE BLACK PEARL

Music by Klaus Badelt

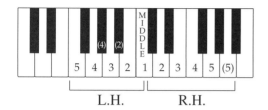

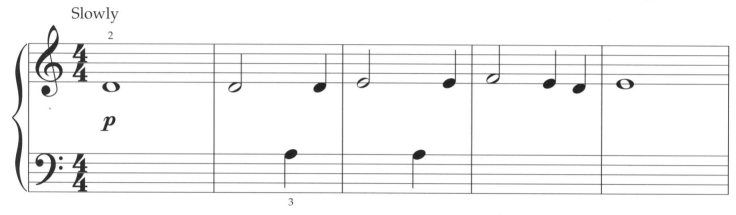

Duet Part (Student plays one octave higher than written.)

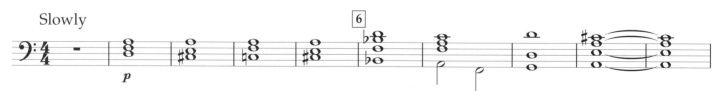

© 2003 Walt Disney Music Company
All Rights Reserved   Used by Permission

Slightly faster

Slightly faster

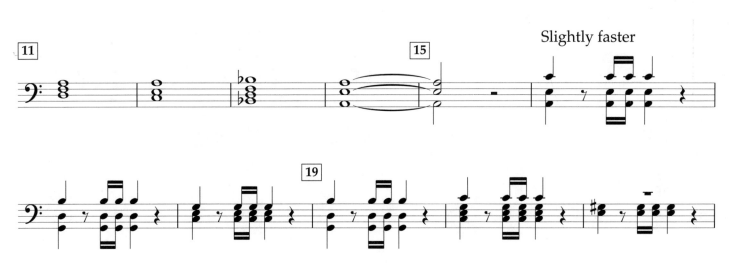

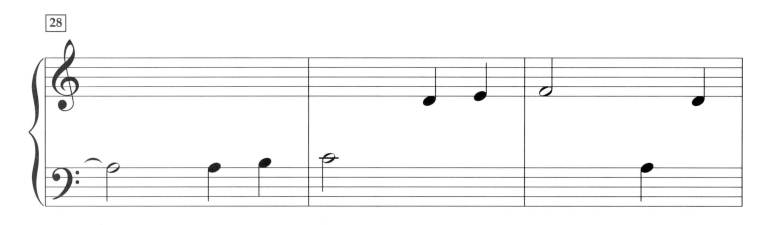

Davy Jones Plays His Organ

from Walt Disney Pictures' PIRATES OF THE CARIBBEAN: DEAD MAN'S CHEST

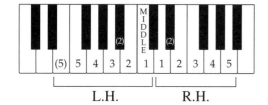

Music by Hans Zimmer

Quickly

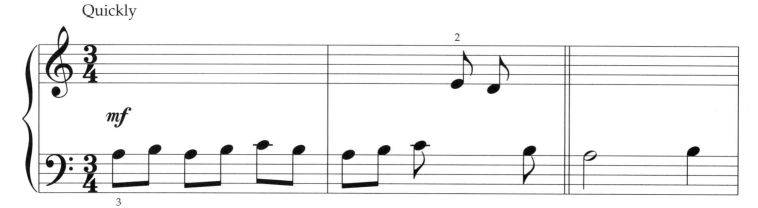

Duet Part (Student plays one octave higher than written.)

Quickly

© 2006 Walt Disney Music Company
All Rights Reserved   Used by Permission

He's a Pirate
from Walt Disney Pictures' PIRATES OF THE CARIBBEAN:
THE CURSE OF THE BLACK PEARL

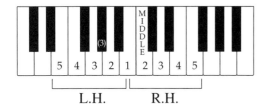

Music by Klaus Badelt

Briskly

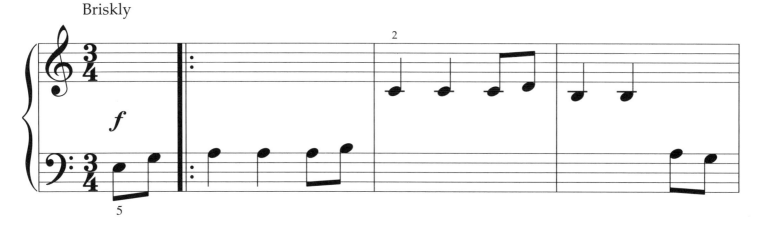

Duet Part (Student plays one octave higher than written.)

Briskly

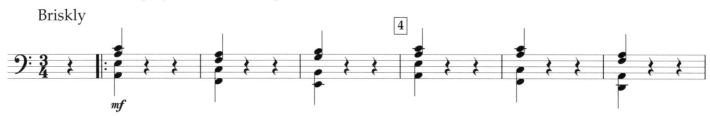

© 2003 Walt Disney Music Company
All Rights Reserved   Used by Permission

(3)

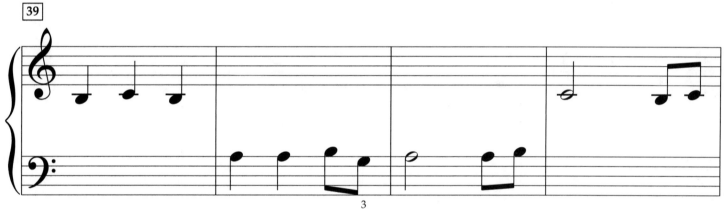

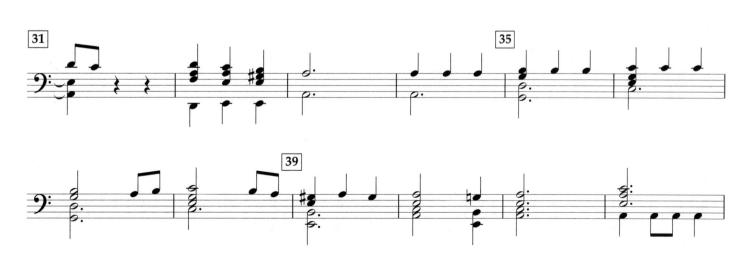

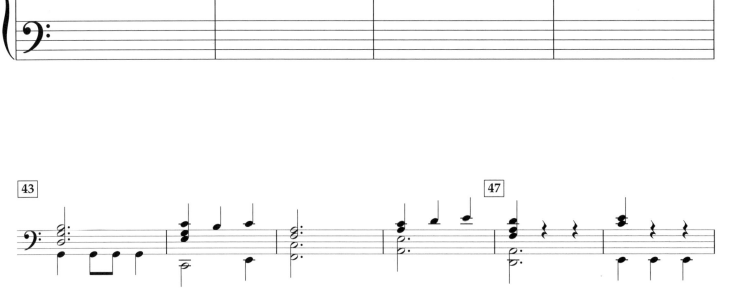

21

Hoist the Colours
from Walt Disney Pictures' PIRATES OF THE CARIBBEAN: AT WORLD'S END

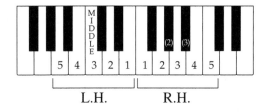

Lyrics by Ted Elliot and Terry Rossio
Music by Hans Zimmer and Gore Verbinski

Moderately slow

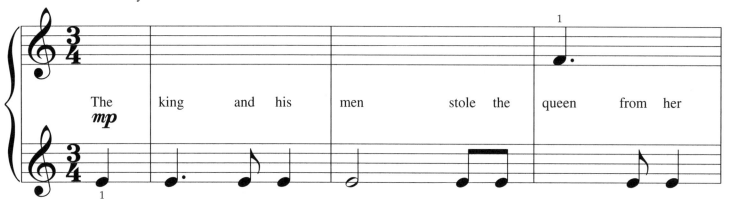

The king and his men stole the queen from her

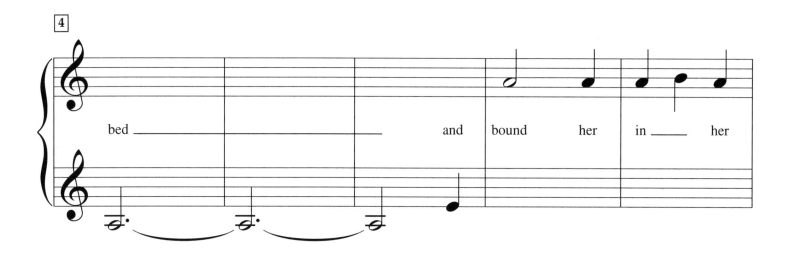

bed and bound her in her

Duet Part (Student plays as written.)

Moderately slow

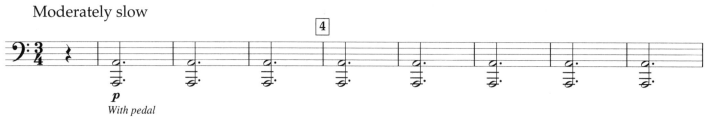

p
With pedal

© 2007 Walt Disney Music Company and Wonderland Music Company, Inc.
All Rights Reserved   Used by Permission

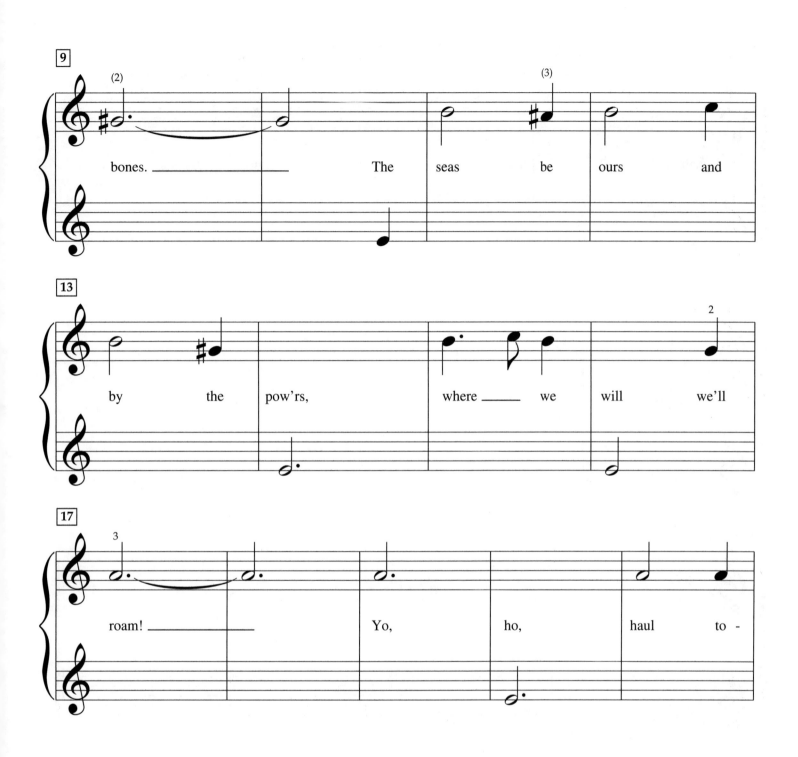

bones. _____ The seas be ours and

by the pow'rs, where ___ we will we'll

roam! _____ Yo, ho, haul to -

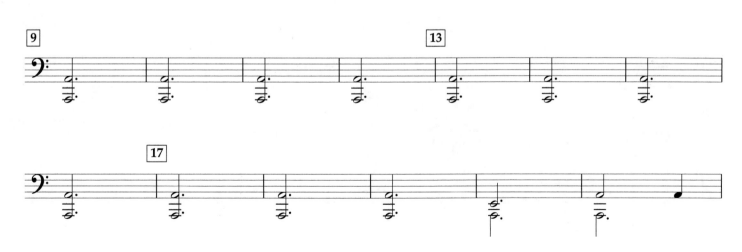

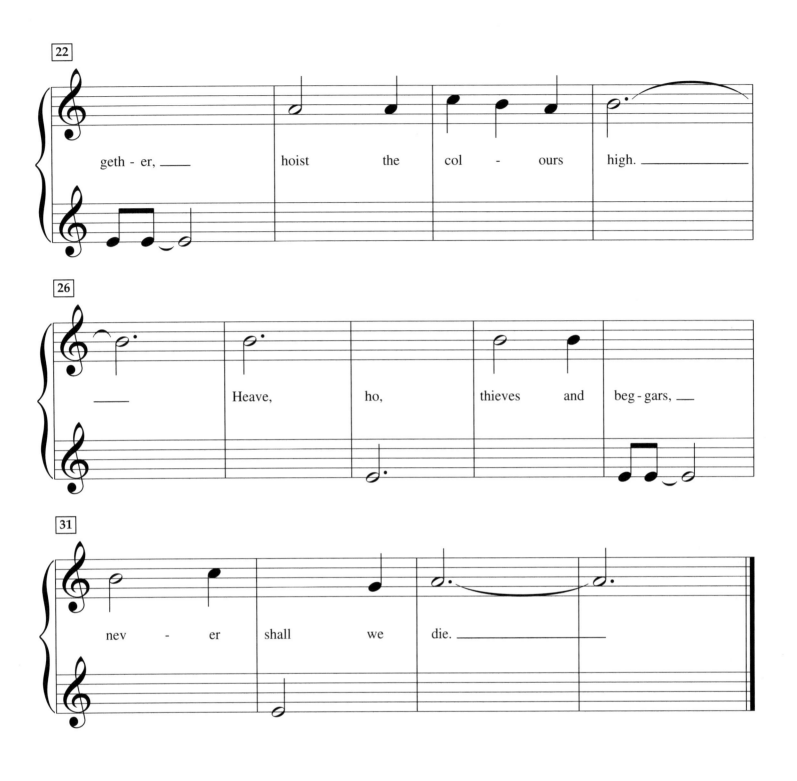

The Medallion Calls
from Walt Disney Pictures' PIRATES OF THE CARIBBEAN:
THE CURSE OF THE BLACK PEARL

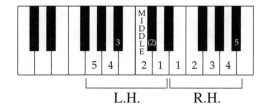

Music by Klaus Badelt

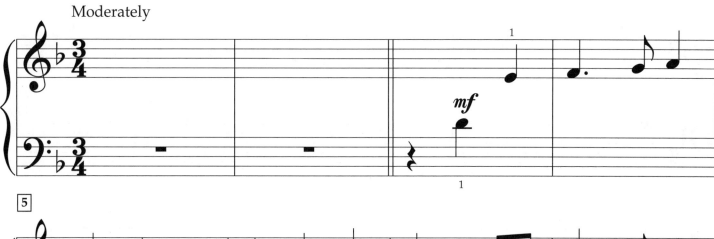

Duet Part (Student plays one octave higher than written.)

© 2003 Walt Disney Music Company
All Rights Reserved   Used by Permission

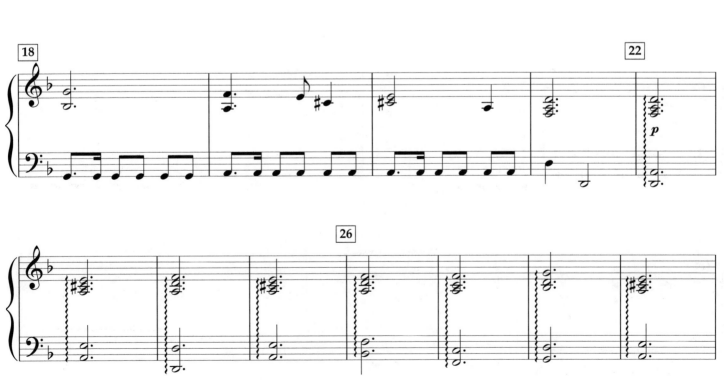

27

Up Is Down

from Walt Disney Pictures' PIRATES OF THE CARIBBEAN: AT WORLD'S END

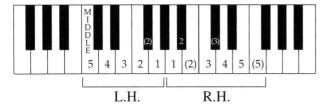

Music by Hans Zimmer

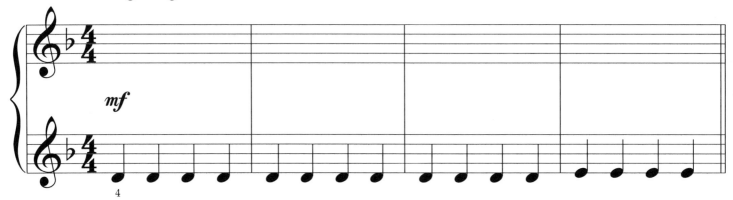

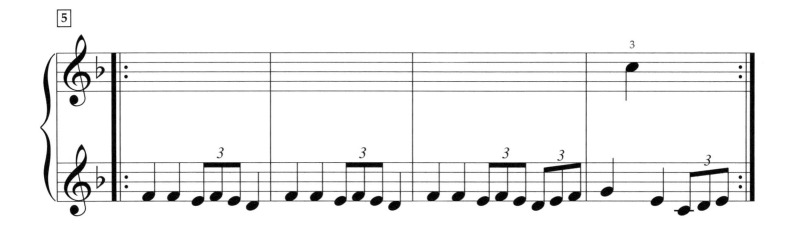

Duet Part (Student plays as written.)

© 2007 Walt Disney Music Company
All Rights Reserved   Used by Permission

32

One Day

from Walt Disney Pictures' PIRATES OF THE CARIBBEAN: AT WORLD'S END

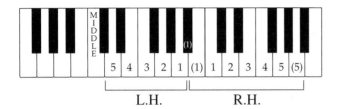

Music by Hans Zimmer

Slowly

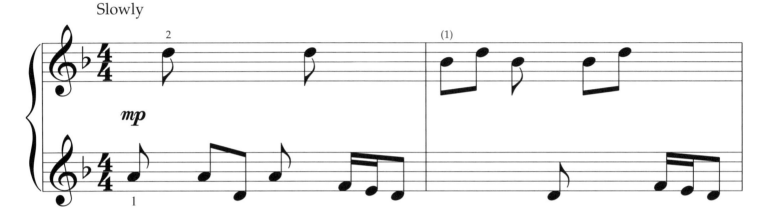

Duet Part (Student plays as written.)

Slowly

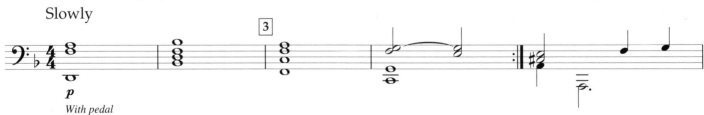

With pedal

© 2007 Walt Disney Music Company
All Rights Reserved   Used by Permission

PLAYING PIANO HAS NEVER BEEN EASIER!

5-FINGER PIANO COLLECTIONS FROM HAL LEONARD

BEATLES! BEATLES!

8 classics, including: A Hard Day's Night • Hey Jude • Love Me Do • P.S. I Love You • Ticket to Ride • Twist and Shout • Yellow Submarine • Yesterday.

_____ 00292061 ....$8.99

CHILDREN'S TV FAVORITES

Themes from 8 Hit Shows

Five-finger arrangements of the themes for: Barney • Bob the Builder • Thomas the Tank Engine • Dragon Tales • PB&J Otter • SpongeBob SquarePants • Rugrats • Dora the Explorer.

_____ 00311208 ....$7.95

CHURCH SONGS FOR KIDS

Features five-finger arrangements of 15 sacred favorites, including: Amazing Grace • The B-I-B-L-E • Down in My Heart • Fairest Lord Jesus • Hallelu, Hallelujah! • I'm in the Lord's Army • Jesus Loves Me • Kum Ba Yah • My God Is So Great, So Strong and So Mighty • Oh, How I Love Jesus • Praise Him, All Ye Little Children • Zacchaeus • and more.

_____ 00310613 .... $7.95

CLASSICAL FAVORITES – 2ND EDITION

arr. Carol Klose

Includes 12 beloved classical pieces from Bach, Bizet, Haydn, Grieg and other great composers: Bridal Chorus • Hallelujah! • He Shall Feed His Flock • Largo • Minuet in G • Morning • Rondeau • Surprise Symphony • To a Wild Rose • Toreador Song.

_____ 00310611 .... $7.95

CONTEMPORARY MOVIE HITS – 2ND EDITION

7 favorite songs from hit films: Go the Distance (Hercules) • My Heart Will Go On (Titanic) • When You Believe (The Prince of Egypt) • You'll Be in My Heart (Tarzan™) • You've Got a Friend in Me (Toy Story and Toy Story II) • more.

_____ 00310687 ....$7.95

DISNEY MOVIE FUN

8 classics, including: Beauty and the Beast • When You Wish Upon a Star • Whistle While You Work • and more.

_____ 00292067 .... $7.95

DISNEY TUNES

Includes: Can You Feel the Love Tonight? • Chim Chim Cher-ee • Go the Distance • It's a Small World • Supercalifragilisticexpialidocious • Under the Sea • You've Got a Friend in Me • Zero to Hero.

_____ 00310375 .... $7.95

SELECTIONS FROM DISNEY'S PRINCESS COLLECTION VOL. 1

7 songs sung by Disney heroines – with a full-color illustration of each! Includes: Colors of the Wind • A Dream Is a Wish Your Heart Makes • I Wonder • Just Around the Riverbend • Part of Your World • Something There • A Whole New World.

_____ 00310847 ....$7.95

EENSY WEENSY SPIDER & OTHER NURSERY RHYME FAVORITES

Includes 11 rhyming tunes kids love: Hickory Dickory Dock • Humpty Dumpty • Hush, Little Baby • Jack and Jill • Little Jack Horner • Mary Had a Little Lamb • Peter, Peter Pumpkin Eater • Pop Goes the Weasel • Tom, Tom, the Piper's Son • more.

_____ 00310465 .... $7.95

GOD BLESS AMERICA®

8 PATRIOTIC AND INSPIRATIONAL SONGS

Features 8 patriotic favorites anyone can play: America, the Beautiful • Battle Hymn of the Republic • God Bless America • My Country, 'Tis of Thee (America) • The Star Spangled Banner • This Is My Country • This Land Is Your Land • You're a Grand Old Flag.

_____ 00310828 .... $7.95

MOVIE MAGIC – 2ND EDITION

Seven gems from the silver screen arranged for beginners. Includes: Chariots of Fire • (Everything I Do) I Do It for You • Heart and Soul • I Will Always Love You • The Rainbow Connection • Summer Nights • Unchained Melody.

_____ 00310261 .... $7.95

THE SOUND OF MUSIC

8 big-note arrangements of popular songs from this perennial favorite musical, including: Climb Ev'ry Mountain • Do-Re-Mi • Edelweiss • The Lonely Goatherd • My Favorite Things • Sixteen Going on Seventeen • So Long, Farewell • The Sound of Music.

_____ 00310249 ....$9.99

HAL•LEONARD® CORPORATION

7777 W. BLUEMOUND RD. P.O. BOX 13819 MILWAUKEE, WI 53213

www.halleonard.com

Disney characters and artwork © Disney Enterprises, Inc.

Prices, contents and availability subject to change without notice.

HAL LEONARD
Beginning Piano Solo Play-Along

The Beginning Piano Solo Play-Along series is designed for pianists ready to play their first solo. Each volume comes with a CD of orchestrated arrangements. The music in the books match these recorded orchestrations, and are carefully arranged for beginning pianists. There are two tracks: a full performance track for listening and practice, plus a separate backing track that lets you be the soloist! The CDs are playable on any CD player, and are also enhanced so Mac and PC users can adjust the recording to any tempo without changing the pitch.

1. Disney Favorites
Can You Feel the Love Tonight • If I Never Knew You (Love Theme from Pocahontas) • Mickey Mouse March • Supercalifragilisticexpialidocious • When She Loved Me • A Whole New World • You Can Fly! You Can Fly! You Can Fly! • Zip-A-Dee-Doo-Dah
00316163 Book/CD Pack $14.99

2. The Beatles Hits
And I Love Her • Eight Days a Week • Good Night • Hey Jude • Let It Be • When I'm Sixty-Four • Yellow Submarine • Yesterday
00316164 Book/CD Pack $14.99

3. The Sound of Music
Climb Ev'ry Mountain • Do-Re-Mi • Edelweiss • The Lonely Goatherd • Maria • My Favorite Things • Sixteen Going on Seventeen • So Long, Farewell
00316165 Book/CD Pack $14.99

4. Christmas Hits
Christmas Time Is Here • A Holly Jolly Christmas • Jolly Old St. Nicholas • Let It Snow! Let It Snow! Let It Snow! • O Christmas Tree • Rudolph the Red-Nosed Reindeer • Silver Bells • White Christmas
00316166 Book/CD Pack $14.99

5. Christmas Classics
The First Noel • Jingle Bells • Joy to the World • O Come, All Ye Faithful (Adeste Fideles) • Silent Night • Up on the Housetop • We Wish You a Merry Christmas • What Child Is This?
00312193 Book/CD Pack $14.99

6. Disney Hits
Alice in Wonderland • Beauty and the Beast • Bibbidi-Bobbidi-Boo (The Magic Song) • Chim Chim Cher-ee • Circle of Life • It's a Small World • Written in the Stars • You've Got a Friend in Me
00316167 Book/CD Pack $14.99

7. The Beatles Favorites
All My Loving • Blackbird • Good Day Sunshine • Here, There and Everywhere • I Want to Hold Your Hand • In My Life • Michelle • Something
00307288 Book/CD Pack $14.99

8. Andrew Lloyd Webber
All I Ask of You • Any Dream Will Do • As If We Never Said Goodbye • Learn to Be Lonely • Love Changes Everything • Make up My Heart • Memory • Unexpected Song
00307304 Book/CD $14.99

9. Standards
Beyond the Sea • Blue Skies • In the Mood • It Might As Well Be Spring • Mairzy Doats • Moon River • The Surrey with the Fringe on Top • Unchained Melody
00312253 Book/CD Pack $14.99

FOR MORE INFORMATION, SEE YOUR LOCAL MUSIC DEALER, OR WRITE TO:

HAL•LEONARD®
CORPORATION
7777 W. BLUEMOUND RD. P.O. BOX 13819 MILWAUKEE, WI 53213

www.halleonard.com

Disney characters and artwork © Disney Enterprises, Inc.
Prices, contents and availability subject to change without notice.